For When Your Thoughts Are Burning

Ideas and Reminders for a
Less Brutal Existence

About this Book

During the loneliest, most anxiety-inducing time of my life, my own heartbeat would startle me awake at night.

It was the spring of 2020, and I was 24. I was living alone: No partner, no pet, 2,000 miles from family. All but one of my friends had ghosted, moved, or become unavailable. I was finishing my first degree online, working part-time as a barista in a restaurant during the throes of essential work, and writing and releasing long-awaited music projects to distant audiences I'd never quite reach.

This book is:
The reminders I had posted on my refrigerator, on my mirror—the kind I'd normally take down when company came over, but no one ever came over; the notifications I had set up in the Reminders app on my phone; the quotes I'd stick in the back of my deliberately-transparent phone case; the letters I'd keep in my work locker. When I say these pages literally kept me going, I mean literally in the literal sense of the word. These reminders, affirmations, and thoughts rewired my neural pathways during a period of un-magical thinking. I became one with these words and that's how I made it through.

Since late 2020, curiosity as a means to authenticity has become my modus operandi. We're all capable of becoming new each day. We're all capable of change if change is what we're seeking. I became someone entirely new. I became this book.

24 is a rollercoaster year, whether you're ensconced in global trauma or not. And as the world continues to operate in extremes, I hope this bedside table book will be helpful to have. If you're setting a boundary or apologizing for one, exiting or reentering your old life, I hope rewiring your thoughts with the insights in these simple words facilitates a less brutal, more authentic existence.

For me, the spine of this book became the backbone I never had.

The goal isn't to heal forever.
The goal is to heal enough.

Perfect is the opposite of authentic.
One contains magnetism and magic.
One is a black hole of inadequacy.
Choose wisely.

Stop trying to be someone else.
Trying to be some other way.
Comparing, caring, trying to fit in, to change.
Stop.
Stop wasting energy. Time.
Be <u>how you are</u>. Period.
Full stop.
The rest will fall into place.

We're not confident where we're not comfortable.
The incessant test of life is to learn to feel

confident
and competent

regardless of comfort.

See how long you can filter your thoughts
into two categories:
Stillness and kindness.
Not long? Try again. Not long? Try again.
Keep going.
No one can change your inner dialogue but you.

It helps to remember that nothing *requires* freaking out.

Nothing.

When you're inauthentic,
you deny yourself the opportunity to connect.

For example, there was a time I was embarrassed to tell my hair stylist
where I lived while spending so much money on hair color.

Little did I know, we were neighbors.

Trust that it's right.

Shift your inner dialogue
from critical and questioning
to compassionate and accepting.

Being as perfect as possible
and never ruffling any feathers,
rocking any boats
will ultimately
cause you to lose your mind,
resent the feathers,
sink the boat.

You're running low, honey.

Take the power cord out of society and social media and reality TV and your grandmother's expectations,

and plug it back into yourself.

Don't trust yourself?
Cool.

People will leech on that until
your identity disappears altogether.

And as someone who's been through it,

trust me when I say it's much harder
to build self-trust when
you have no idea who you've become or
how you got there.

Lean in.

Turn towards.

Stop waiting for your life to begin.

It already has, honey.
It already has honey.

You don't have to tailor your answers to who you're talking to.

Just be who you are, dammit.

A Note About Boundaries:

Instead of changing the framework
of a relationship once you're in it,
be authentic from the beginning.
Don't set a precedent
you'd hate or resent to maintain.

Here's a thought:
Stop Googling shit.

The stranger on the forum that answered
a vaguely similar question seven years ago
may certainly be an expert about your
particular life scenario,
but what do you think?

What do *you* think?

You don't have to be the one who always answers.
You don't have to be the one who always gives.
The one who's uncomfortable.
You. Don't. Have. To.

Chill, child.

It's just a day.
It's *just* a day.
It's just *a* day.

It's just a *day*.

It's okay to hold still within yourself.
It's okay to be content for one second,
one year, however long.
It's okay to feel good.
To let yourself be content.
To hold a moment.
To hold still.

Hold.

It's your life, not your life sentence.

When you feel physically stuck on your couch and too overwhelmed
to even just stand—get up.
Just get up.
Don't wait for the feeling.
Recognize the inability as the stimulus to kick in the reinforcements.
And the reinforcements are simply you saying to yourself—maybe
out loud—okay, now we get up.
And get up.

This may seem trivial
until you find yourself in the situation.

A life is a responsibility.
It's worthy.
Take it on.

It might still hurt, but
it won't feel better once you beat yourself up again for it.

Wounds that you accept and tend to
have a better chance of healing
than wounds you continually bash into a wall.

Brutal, huh?

Remember resilience?
Remember what *creates* resilience?

You decide what you're comfortable
being uncomfortable with.

It's a matter of self-trust strength training.

You can choose to be louder.
You can choose to be softer.

Electric?
Easeful.

Sometimes thinking you have a problem
and trying to figure that out
is the problem.

Tiny nothings have a tendency
to coup d'état
your whole day.

Anticipate this
with emotional armor in hand.

Stop asking yourself what's wrong with you
and
start asking what's wrong with your circumstances.

Lean towards nuances, not extremes.
It's not always sink or swim.
Sometimes you have the choice to just ... float.

It all worked out the way it had to because of the elements of the situation and the people involved.
You don't blame lithium and nitrogen for exploding.
Some things are fine on their own, but lethal together.
Some things are great on their own,
and even better together.

You can't know until you know.

It's typically advisable
to compromise an outside relationship
before you compromise your relationship
with yourself.

Assume there's a reason
you can't
do things differently
yet.

Note to self when the alarm clock tolls:
Good morning and please get out of your own damn way.

Choose your inner child not your inner critic.
Every time.
No excuses.

Assume position
as a visible, accountable human being
with your own karma and choices.

The minute you start choosing yourself,
the world starts mirroring that back to you.

You have the power to choose your reframe.

A reminder to prioritize proper sleep.

Good sleep can help us
process, sort, and calm our thoughts.

By some magic, sometimes we even wake up knowing the answers.

There are phases where I find I don't actually
want to do *anything.*

Sometimes it's just about getting started.
That I don't want to do the thing until I'm doing it.
And then it's fine.

Other times,
I get started and actually
despise the thing even more.

But I always feel better after.

Let the afterglow keep you motivated.
Keep you aligned.
Sometimes that's all we have
until we feel like ourselves again.

Accept the damn compliment.

Only ever go inward

with compassion.

ONLY EVER GO INWARD

WITH COMPASSION.

Please don't fight your life.

Don't act from the anxious, people-pleasing place.

Find your ocean.
Find your calm.
Your inner endless
ocean of calm.

Act from that space.

If you experience a betrayal of some kind,
it becomes easy to get lost in your mind.

Instead,
try to simply work on being the most trustworthy, loyal person.

Despite it all.

Don't focus on what someone else is doing.
What someone else did.
Focus on putting your trust in yourself.

<u>Don't build a wall, fill the well.</u>

1 + 2 does not equal c.
Don't assume.
Don't convolute.

Whose thoughts are those, really?
Do you recognize that voice?

If it isn't your own, what's it doing in your head
narrating your thoughts, feelings,
each and every move?

I once heard that changing your habits
is much easier when it's a matter of what you
do and don't do.

Not a matter of what you *should* do.
Not a matter of what you *can* do.
Just a matter of what you – *do*.

Your resentment
is proportional to
your boundaries.

Don't make other people's
schedules and priorities
your schedule and priority.

Say no.

Their priorities become your distractions.

You can't get what you want out of *your* day
if it's filled with *their* life.

Your failure to validate
your thoughts and feelings
amplifies them, FYI.

And it doesn't do anyone
any good
to behave from an exaggerated place.

The idea that you can know without knowing.

If you're stuck in a habit of ruminating on your bad days
—complaining and repeating, complaining and repeating—
my advice is to document your good days.

All the details.

What time did you wake up? Who did you talk to?
Who didn't you talk to? What did you do? Where did you go?

Write it all down.

Do this often.
Document the good
and incorporate it into your day.

Make *this* your new mindless habit.

Don't waste your time analyzing
somebody else's situation.

Don't ruminate on it. Don't compare.

Are you involved in the situation?

Fine,
then use your confusion as a chance to connect with the person and
try to understand them better.

Otherwise,
simply let it be with grace.

This approach to other people's business
will significantly
elevate your inner peace.

Focus on
how you want to *feel*.

Lean towards
"inclined to"
and away from
"supposed to."

Your anxiety is
telling you something.
Learn when to listen.

The internal conflict you feel daily over how you think you're
supposed to _____
is draining your energy.
Thinning your hair.
Stressing you out.
Wasting your time.
Blocking your blessings.
Clouding your view.
Killing you, frankly.

Comparison has a tendency
to
slowly but surely

eat us alive.

Breathe into who. you. are.

Your focus in every interaction,
every emotion, every situation,
every MINUTE
is fostering trust in yourself.

Breathing trust and presence into every instance.

When you're in a negative state,
and finally understand something
or see something for what it is
or feel the need to make a life change or scream…
know that it isn't real.

Strong emotions that facilitate complete and sudden understanding
aren't real.
Balance and logic are real.
Don't make a decision from a place of pain.
Lie down on the floor and calm down.
It will pass.
Maybe in minutes, maybe in days.
Maybe longer.

But for god's sake,
don't do anything of significance with urgency.

What I'd Tell My Twenty-Year-Old Self:

You will make money
and you will find love
due to your authenticity
and level of self-love, compassion, and respect.
Not due to your pain-motivation
and intense longing
to stop that discomfort.

Secrecy
facilitates
perfectionism.

What No One Told Me About Boundaries:

If you've been a people-pleaser for a while or forever, the first boundary you set in each relationship will probably not be well-received.

You might be thinking,
"Great, you just made this even harder."
But actually, I'm saving you months of self-flagellation and shame.
If you're respectful and conscientious in setting your boundary, the other person's reaction has nothing to do with you.

Remember, the people we gravitated towards as people-pleasers also gravitated towards us.
They were looking for someone to bend to their every whim.

The stronger their reaction to a conscientious boundary, the more indicative of the kind of friend they were to you.

Do not let their reaction bully you back into place.
Stand your ground. And if necessary, walk away.

Sometimes all you have to do
is the opposite of what
you normally would.

Have you tried <u>that</u> yet?

It helps
to have some knowledge
of your emotional distortions.

Breathe in
peace and grace.

Breathe out
turbulence and insecurity.

Take in
s p a c e,

let go of
scarcity.

Your ability to matter is not conditional.

Choose to focus on gratitude.
And don't forget the because.

I am grateful for _____ because _____.

Because is key.

This becomes especially first-aid-like
when you're hyperventilating
on the bathroom floor.

Compassion, gentleness, and patience
are the balm to your anxiety.

Hold yourself closer
when you feel an
emotional storm
coming.

Be more committed
to the fulfilment of your potential
than to what others think of you.

Give yourself permission
to stop neurotically obsessing
over yourself and your situation.

Sometimes you literally (*literally*) have to
stop mid-sentence, close the browser,
hang up the phone, walk away from the mirror and say—
~~sorry~~, decide—
nope, we don't do that anymore.

I hereby forfeit
my anxious point of view on life
and swear to relax,
put in an honest effort,
and trust with patience.

There were times I got through
simply by asking myself,
"What would a person who's *not* depressed do?"

Picture your inner child and ask them what they're needing in this moment.

You Are Not A Cat

Some of us have had so many negative experiences that we've
become stoic and untrusting.
Perfectly still like soldiers on guard.

Meanwhile our insides are curious and anxious and feeling and
wondering.

As the fable *actually* says,
curiosity is the means toward satisfaction.
You are a conscious, social creature.
Each time you lose, you gain wisdom.
You gain life.

Your curiosity will not kill you,
it might just breathe in some new perspective.
And new perspective might allow you to begin a whole new chapter.
And a whole new chapter begins a whole new life.
Over and over and over and over and over and over and over and over and over.
Nine lives, nine beginnings.

Go for a walk.
Go for multiple walks.

Fresh air, fresh mind.

A helpful tool is to take the action that the person who you want to be would take.

For example: Would the person who you want to be turn on *Golden Girls* reruns at 2 p.m. on a Monday, or would she start her manuscript? Would the person who you want to be habitually eat a salad or habitually eat a cheeseburger?

I'm not saying one choice is obviously
wrong or right.
I'm just saying one might be more aligned
for who you want to be.

And all we can really do is aim to make a good percentage of aligned choices and raise that percentage each and every day.

(Or maybe just maintain an agreeable percentage.)

Sometimes we have to use logic over feeling.
Especially when we are stuck.

A weird trick to get out of victim mentality
is to choose a sickening amount of self-pride.

You cannot play the victim regarding outcomes
of choices you made with absolute fortitude.

Did they really waste your time, or
did you know better
and waste your own time?

You don't need to be meaner
or harder,
just honest.

Struggle
is the only prerequisite
for *resilience*.

Perseverance
is the only requisite
for *triumph*.

Sometimes going to bed early
and sleeping in
has the rejuvenating
effect of a getaway.

Don't underestimate this.

You are entitled to act differently
towards people who hurt you and didn't apologize.

Holding someone accountable
is not the same
as holding a grudge.

Holding a grudge
is not the same
as holding someone accountable.

You are well-spoken, so speak well.

You don't sleep in the same sheets forever.
You don't resent your kitchen sink for getting dirty.

You might hate laundry, dishes, etc.
But you don't expect them to take care of themselves.

The same applies to mental well-being.

Practice mindful emotional upkeep.
No matter how much maintenance.
Your mind is the only home you've got.

Make it a nice place to live.

The inner voice that's the antithesis of balance is your downfall.
You know the one.

Your Achilles heel. Your inner critic.
Name it.
I mean it—name it.

Pick your least favorite character.
Or pick a name you hate.

Instead of calling your mom crying from the bathroom floor because
your life has no meaning and your hair is awful and you have no
friends and you can't make rent and you don't know your purpose,
you can just say,
"Ohhhh. Bellatrix, you're back."

Things are less scary when they can be called by name.

When you're flailing... unsettled and desperate... when you would typically do that thing that you'll regret later... that toxic behavior, bad habit, you know the one... instead,
visualize your ideal self slowly morphing and filling in every last color and contour of your body.

Recognize how deep you go.
How much room you have for good feelings, bad feelings, relationships, successes, big life moments.
Breathe through the pressure. See yourself as bigger.
See yourself as capable.

See yourself in the context of your life.

And make the choice from that capable place.

This is your one and only life.
For god's sake,
no flailing.

That balmy warmth you feel
when you take a deep breath in?
That's what you want your life to feel like.

That's what you want your life
to breathe back into you.

Instead of pursuing those who avoid you,
receive those who show up for you.

Oh, you seem to think you have no one?
Someone will come.

But only if you show up for yourself first.

Are you behaving inconsequentially and invisibly
because you know you actually have a tremendous effect?

How do we own that effect?
How do we shift that behavior?

When you are in the process of getting your life together,
you might feel motivated to get up earlier.

This can be hysterically challenging.
Yes, I'm laughing at you.

What helped me was to
remember how I wanted to feel.

And there is nothing more miserable than starting your day with an
internal battle.
And someone laughing at you.

So when you hear that alarm, act on habit.
Default mode. Factory settings.

Don't involve pity, trust, gentleness.
Just wake up. Just get the f up.

Refuse to beat yourself up for not knowing the solution.

Nope, I don't care if it is a practical problem.

The answer will come to you
when your mind is
regulated, calm,
kind, and clear.

Not in the midst of an attack.

I used to be terrified of engulfment by other people.
Learning about another's interests, hobbies, job, life
quite literally felt like a blow to my identity.

After a period of solitude,
I ventured back into the world.

It was still challenging.

But *people* are our greatest tests.
Our reaction to *people* tells us all we need to know.

Take some time to be alone.
Then venture into the world.
And while you're out there, set boundaries, trust yourself,
accept yourself.
Set boundaries again.
And again.

This isn't a total fix for your problems,
but it is a remedy for you in the context of real life.
We can't all be a monk in a house on a hill.

Sometimes it's helpful to use challenging family relationships as a meditation exercise.

The ultimate Olympic training of Zen.

You can't always eliminate the trigger,
but you can always change your perception.

*Read Dr. Edith Eger's story if you doubt this.

Meditation brings forward that juxtaposition
of hyper-awareness and hyper-relaxation.

Also known as *presence*.

Ah, the ability to respond to life as if in slow motion,
at your own casual pace,
where you're always right on time.

Be bolder.

Just answer the question
whatever the answer may be.
That's your truth.

Isn't that worth something?

Your truth should be worth something to you.

To my fellow people-pleasers:

Remember that during each interaction you are an equal participant/player.

Ready player one?
(We are all player one.)

You're wasting time
worrying about
what hasn't happened yet.

Just be present.

Judging yourself or beating yourself up
will not get you anywhere faster;
but showing up to the day and tasks at hand—
setting meaningful goals that you consistently meet
will.

One time I repeated, "My feelings are justified," every morning in the mirror for three months.

And then in the heat of an argument with
a toxic person who was gaslighting me,
I blurted out,
"My feelings are valid! Everything I'm saying is justified."

And they actually got quiet and said,
"Yeah, you're right."

When you hit rock bottom,
your affirmations become your backbone.

Sometimes just taking a shower

s l o w s

the
whole
damn

s p i r a l.

People's opinions of you are not the law.

People's opinions of you are not necessarily
even based in reality.

What other people do and say is
a reflection of them, not you.

If someone questions you or your choices,
and you aren't causing (avoidable) harm,
your job is to simply and wholeheartedly declare,

"It's my life! I trust my choices!"

When I was low on self-belief,
I made it a goal to align with the dream result instead
of the potential rejection.
For instance, instead of talking myself out of sending the email
because of how painful it'd be to not hear back for the hundredth
time,
I sent the email for how good it'd feel to hear back once.

*This does not apply to exes

You're allowed to have an opinion.
You're allowed to have interests.
You're allowed to have needs.
You're allowed to have wants.

People who don't want you to have an opinion, needs, wants, interests...
a voice...

Well, they sound dull and impossible.

Ask questions.
Be accountable for the people you allow into your life.

I once found myself in a car to Joshua Tree because I hadn't asked my friends what we were doing that evening. I assumed maybe dinner.

I once found myself being screamed at by a childhood friend that I hadn't talked to in years. I'd found it odd that she was calling, and really didn't have the time or energy to chat. But I answered anyway and paid the price.

I once found myself dumped by a boyfriend who had recently started medication for a psychological disorder after being manic through the course of our entire relationship. I had no idea any of this was going on.

In each case, I had no concept of the plot of my own story.

Ask questions.
Don't make yourself resolutely, unconditionally
loyal and available.

Listen to that inner voice.

It's a token of self-respect, a builder of self-trust to know what situations you're voluntarily choosing to put yourself in.

Finish these sentences:

The person I want to be is...
The person I want to be does...
The person I want to be has...
The person I want to be feels...
The person I want to be forgives...
The person I want to be lets go of...

Even when it feels like the world is happening *to* you,
you get to choose your experience.

The mind is incredibly powerful.

You may not always be able to stay in your power,
but you're always able to guard your spirit.

Can you steal a fraction of your power back
by retreating into your mind?
By turning inward?

What's special about starting small is that before you make the
change, it feels simultaneously pointless and impossible...

But once you've conquered a seemingly minuscule mountain,
you feel like the king of the world.

Yeah, king.

Be gentle enough with yourself
that your inner child feels safe
to peak out sometimes and say hello.

You'll feel it when it happens.

It may take a while.

She's fine. He's fine. I'm fine.
Let it lie. Let it flow. Let them be.

A mantra for when you're stuck
in a cynical, judgmental thought loop.
Or maybe just refreshing
a human or Internet gossip funnel.

There was an entire year that I only made it through by staring at myself in the mirror each day and repeating:

This is temporary. My circumstances will change.

Repeat as needed.
Or do with it what you will.

Is there an action you can take that will move you
one inch closer to your ideal?

Or are you forcing control and perfectionism
over yourself and your surroundings?

Whatever you had to suppress growing up
is probably wildly triggering to you right now.

For instance,
if you were emotionally neglected as a child,
you might feel trapped and scared when
you find somewhere you belong.

Being part of something, feeling cherished and loved... might not
come naturally to you.

I know I felt safer alone
when all I wanted was connection.

We play tricks on ourselves
until we grow our self-awareness.
And maybe even learn
to outsmart our minds.

If you're in a rut,
begin your day with a walk.

Consistently instilling rhythm first thing
eventually turns into a balmy cadence
that lightens your whole day...

and carries you forward.

The things that you struggle so hard with
and feel so much shame about
but cannot
for the life of you
figure out how to fix—
sometimes just cease to exist.

Something changes in your life that eliminates discomfort.
And your coping mechanism becomes eliminated too.
Trust this.

Sometimes the bad just falls away.
But for right now it serves a purpose.

Someday the stuff you're so hyper-focused on
will feel something like
unattainable dust.

Most times, someone can only truly affect you, make you insecure, irritate you, or hurt your feelings if you're already questioning yourself or beating yourself up for that specific thing.

It doesn't mean their behavior is right or cool.

But somewhere within that rough, they've thrown— or rather, chucked—
a diamond at you.

When you're ready, find it.

Tiny Lifehack for Daily Alignment:

Stop watching and reading things just because they're trendy and you want to be in the know.

You will never be able to keep up.

In that regard, just consume what interests you.

There's this saying about perspective.
Something about the forest and the trees.
I'd like to add some perspective to this perspective.

For instance,
let's picture you beating yourself up for releasing your art into the
world and it not being widely received. For neglecting a friend that
bums you out while cultivating a new friendship that feels more
aligned. For waking up later than your goal, but earlier than ever. For
beginning a habit of walking each day, but not coming close to
10,000 steps.

Each aspect is a sign of growth. A tree.
Don't focus on one individual tree—
Its health, height, color.

See yourself for the *forest* you are, not for your specific trees of
accomplishment.
A forest is not about finality or precision.
It's about accumulation.

Are you able to laugh at yourself?

This is important.

If you're feeling resentful,
it may be time to take a closer look
at who or what is
running your show.

Learn to not be affected
by being interrupted or misinterpreted.

Repeat what you said. Say it louder. Lean in.
Ask questions. Listen.

Learn to stay steady in
who you are and how you are
around other people.

You have the choice to
not allow your own insecurities,
or their curiosity or jest
affect your foundation as a human being.

Someday you'll wake up
and find that you exist on the outside
the way you feel on the inside.

And it is more liberating a feeling
than you can possibly imagine.

Literally nobody said it will be easy.

I'm pretty sure everybody actually said
it *won't* be easy.

Anybody who said it *should* be easy
has probably never done it.

They definitely haven't done it in your shoes,
your context.

When things fall into place for somebody,
they tend to preach that their way is
the right way because their way was easy.
For them.

Have you ever considered that maybe they just have lower standards,
not better achievements?

Lower your standards for easy.
Raise your standards for value.

Decide accordingly which applies.
And in which context. *For you.*

(In many cases, fulfilling and aligned is > easy.)

When you stop people-pleasing
and start being genuine,
you might lose a lot of relationships.

When the loneliness kicks in,
I want you to remind yourself not to get swept up
in a spiral of self-blame.
You're not pushing everyone away, or attracting "no one,"
or inviting loneliness into your life.

You're just no longer attracting chaos.

This will feel boring until you recognize
it's actually just sensible.

Someone else's thoughts should not have privilege over your own.

Someone else's opinions should not outrank your inner voice.

Do as you think, not as they say.

My trick for getting out of a negative, analytical, or ruminating thought-loop is to flood my brain with information.

Learn a new language. Listen to a podcast. Immerse yourself in a skill. Find a cause to care about. Volunteer. Read a book. Explore a subject you're passionate about. Make a list of places you want to travel. Cook a meal, bake a cake. Take a tennis lesson.

If all that sounds stupid, watch a movie.

Moral of the story:
Try something new.

Reorient your focus outside yourself.

If you're too careful with yourself, it can backfire.
It can communicate to your brain
that you don't trust yourself.

Find a dispositional balance in which
you're kind and self-soothing,
but still trusting enough in your capabilities
and bravery to do great things.

It's time to accept all the versions of yourself.
That you've ever been. That you are right now.

You are complete and healthiest
when you are balanced, not perfect.

Aim for real. Aim for spice.
Aim for honest.

Not perfectly consistently this way, or that way.
Just real.

Just who you are at this exact millisecond in time.

It took all the mess you've ever been
to get you to this perfectly imperfect place.

You are healing right on time.

About the Author

Callaghan Belle grew up as a child prodigy in various music fields, most notably songwriting, arrangement, and production. She is a Warner Chappell songwriter and has released several albums.

Callaghan holds a dual-BA in psychology and political science from Pennsylvania State University and is currently pursuing her master's degree in clinical psychology at Pepperdine University to become a licensed marriage and family therapist.

She lives in the Beachwood Canyon neighborhood of Los Angeles.

Made in the USA
Middletown, DE
18 November 2024

64864276R00083